For Roberto Clemente
—J. W.

For Lydia Casablanca, whose kindness
and assistance were invaluable
—R. C.

ALADDIN PAPERBACKS
An imprint of Simon & Schuster Children's Publishing Division
1230 Avenue of the Americas, New York, NY 10020
Text copyright © 2005 by Jonah Winter
Illustrations copyright © 2005 by Raúl Colón
All rights reserved, including the right of reproduction in whole or in part in any form.
ALADDIN PAPERBACKS and related logo are registered trademarks of
Simon & Schuster, Inc.
Also available in an Atheneum Books for Young Readers hardcover edition.
Designed by Ann Bobco
The text of this book was set in Palatino.
The illustrations for this book were rendered in watercolor, colored pencils, and litho pencils.
Manufactured in China
First Aladdin Paperbacks edition March 2008
8 10 9 7
The Library of Congress has cataloged the hardcover edition as follows:
Winter, Jonah.
Roberto Clemente : pride of the Pittsburgh Pirates / Jonah Winter ;
illustrated by Raúl Colón.—1st ed.
p. cm.
ISBN-13: 978-0-689-85643-3 (hc.)
ISBN-10: 0-689-85643-1 (hc.)
1. Clemente, Roberto, 1934–1972—Juvenile literature. 2. Baseball players—Puerto Rico—
Biography—Juvenile literature. 3. Pittsburgh Pirates (Baseball team)—Juvenile literature. [1.
Clemente, Roberto, 1934–1972. 2. Baseball players. 3. Puerto Ricans—Biography. 4. Pittsburgh
Pirates (Baseball team)] I. Colón, Raúl, ill. II. Title.
GV865.C45W56 2005
796.357'092—dc22
2003025546
ISBN-13: 978-1-4169-5082-0 (pbk.)
ISBN-10: 1-4169-5082-6 (pbk.)
1111 SCP

ROBERTO

Pride of the Pittsburgh Pirates

CLEMENTE

BY JONAH WINTER

ILLUSTRATED BY

RAÚL COLÓN

Aladdin Paperbacks
New York London Toronto Sydney

On an island called Puerto Rico,
where baseball players are as plentiful

as tropical flowers in a rain forest,
there was a boy who had very little

but a fever to play
and win at baseball.

He had no money for a baseball bat,
so he made one from a guava tree branch.

His first glove he also made,
from the cloth of a coffee-bean sack.

His first baseball field was muddy
and crowded with palm trees.

For batting practice he used empty soup cans
and hit them farther than anyone else.

Soup cans
turned into softballs.

Softballs
turned into baseballs.

Little League turned into
minor league turned into

winter league: professional baseball
in Puerto Rico. He played so well

he received an invitation
to play in . . . the major leagues

in America!
What an honor!

But the young man was sent to a steel-mill town
called Pittsburgh, Pennsylvania,

where his new team, the Pittsburgh Pirates,
was in *last place.*

Now this was something very strange,
being on a losing team.

For the young Puerto Rican,
everything was strange.

Instead of palm trees, he saw smokestacks.
Instead of Spanish, he heard English.

Instead of being *somebody,*
he was nobody.

His first time at bat,
he heard the announcer stumble through his Spanish name:

"ROB, uh, ROE . . . BURRT,
um, let's see, TOE

CLUH-MAINT?"
It echoed in the near-empty stands.

Roberto Clemente was his name,
and this is pronounced "Roe-BEAR-toe Cleh-MEN-tay."

As if to introduce himself,
Roberto *smacked* the very first pitch.

But it went right up the infield . . .
and into the second baseman's glove.

Still, Roberto ran like lightning—
and beat the throw to first base.

The Pittsburgh fans checked their scorecards.
Who was this guy, "Roberto Clemente"?

To his new fans in Pittsburgh,
Roberto was like a jolt of *electricity*.

He could score from first base
on a single.

He could hit line drives,
bunts, towering home runs,

sacrifice flies—
whatever was needed.

Once he even scored an inside-the-park
GRAND SLAM!

Playing right field,
he had no equal.

He was always leaping, diving,
crashing, rolling.

Once, trying to catch a pop fly,
running full speed,

he SLAMMED into the right-field wall—
and fell to the ground.

At last, slowly, he lifted his glove.
The ball was inside.

But it wasn't just how he played.
He had *style*. He was *cool*.

He had this move he did with his neck
before each at bat,

creaking it one way,
then the other.

Soon kids who wanted to be just like Roberto
were doing it too, twisting their necks this way and that.

Roberto did it to ease the pain he felt
from playing his heart out in every game.

"If you don't try as hard as you can," he said,
"you are wasting your life."

Roberto tried so hard,
he helped the last-place Pirates

make it all the way to the World Series
where they beat the mighty NEW YORK YANKEES!

After the series,
down in the streets of Pittsburgh,

Roberto walked alone among his fans,
who were so busy celebrating,

they didn't even notice him.
That didn't bother Roberto.

He was happy to feel lost in the crowd
of a party he had helped create.

But there was something
that would have made Roberto's joy a little sweeter.

As much as fans loved him,
the newspaper writers did not.

When Roberto was in such pain he couldn't play,
they called him "lazy."

They mocked his Spanish accent,
and when Roberto got angry,

the mainly white newsmen
called him a Latino "hothead."

Roberto swore he would be so good,
he would *have* to get the respect he deserved.

He would become the greatest all-around baseball player
there ever was.

At home that Christmas,
Roberto went back to the same muddy field

he'd played on as a boy.
In his pocket was a bag full of bottle caps

that he emptied into the hands of some kids.
They threw him the caps, and he hit each one

again
and again.

When he returned to Pittsburgh come spring,
baseballs looked HUGE,

and he clobbered them as never before.
That season, he hit .351,

the highest batting average
in the National League.

And still he did not get the credit
he deserved for being so great.

"It's because I'm black, isn't it?"
he asked the sneering reporters.

"It's because I am Puerto Rican.
It's because I am proud."

It was starting to seem
as if Roberto might never be respected

in the big world outside of Pittsburgh
and Puerto Rico. And then something happened.

The year was 1971.
The Pirates were in the World Series again,

playing against the Baltimore Orioles,
who were favored to win.

All around America and Puerto Rico,
people sat watching on TV . . .

as Roberto put on a one-man show.
Stealing bases, hitting home runs,

playing right field with a *fire*
most fans had never seen before.

Finally, *finally*,
it could not be denied:

Roberto was the greatest all-around baseball player
of his time, maybe of all time.

The very next year, he did something
that few have ever done:

During the last game of the season,
Roberto walked to the plate,

creaked his neck, dug in his stance,
stuck his chin toward the pitcher,

and walloped a line drive
off the center-field wall—his *three thousandth* hit!

The crowd cheered, and they wouldn't stop cheering.
For many minutes the players stopped playing

and Roberto stood on second base, amazed.
How far he had come.

Roberto is now one of 11 players in major league history to get 3000 or more hits!

And yet, when the season was over,
the hero returned to the place where his story began,

to the land of muddy fields
and soup cans and bottle caps,

to his homeland of Puerto Rico,
where he was worshipped.

But did he sit around
and polish his trophies?

No. That rainy New Year's Eve,
Roberto sat in the San Juan airport

and waited for mechanics to fix the tired old airplane
that would take him to Central America.

There had been a terrible earthquake,
and he wanted to help the victims.

The plane would carry food and supplies
that Roberto had paid for.

Right before midnight, he boarded.
The rain was really coming down.

One of the propellers buzzed loudly.
As the plane took off,

the engines failed
and the plane fell into the ocean.

Just like that, it was over.
Roberto was gone.

How could his story
end this way,

so suddenly,
and with such sadness?

The story doesn't end here.
When someone like Roberto dies,

his spirit lives on
in the hearts of all he touched.

And Roberto's spirit is still growing.
It grows in the bats and gloves

and arms and legs of all the Latino baseball players
who have flooded into the major leagues.

His spirit grows in the charities he started
for poor people in Puerto Rico.

And his spirit is still growing in Pittsburgh,
where people who saw him play

tell their children and grandchildren
of how he used to sparkle—running, diving,

firing game-saving throws
from deep right field

all the way to home plate—
SMACK—right into the catcher's glove.

AUTHOR'S NOTE

Roberto Clemente

(Born on August 18, 1934, in Carolina, Puerto Rico;

died on December 31, 1972, near San Juan, Puerto Rico)

What do people think of when they think of Roberto Clemente? Some baseball fans think of him as "the greatest player who ever lived." They think of his statistics: three thousand hits, twelve Gold Glove awards for his legendary fielding, fourteen All-Star game appearances, a regular-season Most Valuable Player award (1966), a World Series Most Valuable Player award (1971), a .317 lifetime batting average, and the honor of being the first Latino inducted (and in the fastest time ever) into the American Baseball Hall of Fame.

But that's only half the story. When many people hear the name Roberto Clemente, they think of a great *person*. Many people think of a man who died while trying to help earthquake victims. They think of a man who gave much of his money to charities. They think of a man whose money helped to build a sports complex in Puerto Rico for poor children—so they would have the chance to do as he did, to escape poverty through their athletic abilities.

In his native Puerto Rico, Roberto Clemente is still worshipped like a saint. As a husband and father, he is still missed by his wife, Vera, and his three sons, Roberto Jr., Luis Roberto, and Roberto Enrique.